Bodies of Water

Canals

Cassie Mayer

www.heinemann.co.uk/library
Visit our website to find out more information about Heinemann Library books.

To order:
☎ Phone 44 (0) 1865 888066
Send a fax to 44 (0) 1865 314091
📄 Visit the Heinemann Bookshop at www.heinemann.co.uk/library to browse our
💻 catalogue and order online.

First published in Great Britain by Heinemann Library,
Halley Court, Jordan Hill, Oxford OX2 8EJ, part of Harcourt
Education. Heinemann is a registered trademark of Harcourt
Education Ltd.

© Harcourt Education Ltd 2007
First published in paperback in 2008
The moral right of the proprietor has been asserted.

Editorial: Diyan Leake and Cassie Mayer
Design: Joanna Hinton-Malivoire
Picture research: Erica Martin
Production: Duncan Gilbert

Originated by Dot Gradations
Printed and bound in China by South China Printing Co. Ltd

ISBN 978 0 4311 8473 9 (hardback)
11 10 09 08 07
10 9 8 7 6 5 4 3 2 1

ISBN 978 0 4311 8478 4 (paperback)
12 11 10 09 08
10 9 8 7 6 5 4 3 2 1

British Library Cataloguing in Publication Data
Mayer, Cassie
Bodies of Water: Canals

A full catalogue record for this book is available from the British
Library

Acknowledgements
The publishers would like to thank the following for permission
to reproduce photographs: Alamy p. **17** (fstop2); Corbis pp.
4 (NASA), **5** (Free Agents Limited), **10** (Patrick Chauvel),
13 (Alan Schein Photography), **14** (Sergio Pitamitz), **23**
(wide canal: Sergio Pitamitz); FLPA p. **18** (Nigel Cattlin);
Getty Images pp. **6** (Altrendo Travel), **7** (Hulton Archive), **19**
(Photodisc Green), **23** (field: Photodisc Green); Photolibrary
pp. **8** (Herve Gyssels), **9** (Jtb Photo), **11** (Walter Bibikow),
15 (Kindra Clineff), **23** (narrow canal: Kindra Clineff); Robert
Harding pp. **20** (Roy Rainford), **21** (Gavin Hellier), **back
cover** (Kindra Clineff); Waterways Photo Library pp. **12**
(Derek Pratt), **16** (Derek Pratt).

Cover photograph of a canal in Venice, Italy reproduced with
permission of Getty Images/Digital Vision.

Every effort has been made to contact copyright holders of any
material reproduced in this book. Any omissions will be rectified
in subsequent printings if notice is given to the publishers.

Contents

Canals 4

Types of canals 12

What canals do 18

Canal facts. 22

Picture glossary 23

Index 24

Canals

water

Most of the Earth is covered by water.

canal

Some of this water is in canals.

Canals look like rivers but they have straight sides.

Canals are built by people.
They build them in straight lines.

Canals are waterways.

A waterway is like a road.
Boats travel along a waterway.

Canals go through land.

Some canals go through towns
and cities.

Types of canals

Canals can connect rivers.

Some canals connect lakes.

Some canals connect oceans.

Some canals are wide.

Some canals are narrow.

Canals can go down hills.

They have locks to hold the water.

Canals go through tunnels.

What canals do

Canals bring water to land.

The water is used to grow crops.

Canals are used to move
heavy things.

Canals help us move people.

Canal facts

The Grand Canal is the oldest canal. It is in China.

The Grand Canal is also the longest canal.

Picture glossary

 **crop** a plant that is grown for something such as food

 **narrow** short from side to side

 **wide** long from side to side

Index

crop 19

hill 16

lake 12

oceans 13

tunnel 17

Notes for Parents and Teachers

Before reading

Talk to the children about canals. Have they ever seen a canal? How did they know it was a canal and not a river? Explain to them that canals were built by people to take water to different places. Some are large enough to take ships but others are small and just for taking water to the crops. Canals have straight sides and often go in straight lines.

After reading

Dance drama. Play some marching music and tell the children they are going to start by building a canal. Show them how to do digging movements in time to the music. Then say that they are the water in the canal, flowing along and then waiting at a lock before they go down a flight of locks. Finally tell them to be a boat (they should choose what size) and travel along the waterway.

Wide and narrow. Describe wide and narrow canals to the children. When you say the canal is wide, they should open their arms wide; when you say the canal is narrow, they should bring their hands together.

Canal song. To the tune of "We Are Going to the Zoo Tomorrow", make up simple verses for the children to sing; for example, "We are going to the canal tomorrow ... down the lock gates ... through a tunnel".